New Life Clarity Publishing

205 West 300 South, Brigham City, Utah 84302
Http://newlifeclarity.com/

The Right of Ron Britton to be identified as the
Author of the work has been asserted by him in accordance
with the Copyright Act 1988.

New Life Clarity Publishing
name has been established by NLCP.
All Rights Reserved.
No part of this publication may be reproduced, distributed, or
transmitted in any form or by any means, including
photocopying, recording, or other electronic or
mechanical methods without the prior and express
written permission of the author or publisher, except in
the case of brief quotations embodied in critical reviews
and certain other noncommercial uses permitted by
copyright law.

Printed in the United States of America
ISBN- 978-1-0878-7904-8
Copyright@2021 Ron Britton

MEGAS ADELPHOS

Memoirs of a Vet's Mind Wars

Dedication

This book is dedicated to the men and women of the armed forces, those heroes who defended their homeland from both foreign and domestic threats. I wrote this book because I wanted to talk about trauma from many different angles. Trauma comes in many forms, including physical, emotional, and psychological abuse. Military families often experience financial crises that put their mental and physical well-being at risk. The goal of writing this book was to express my concern about vets and their families, and how I feel they should receive all the support we can give them. If even one family member falls through the cracks, the rest of the family suffers with them. I am proud to have served in the United States military. It was one of the greatest choices I have ever made, and I salute every soldier who proudly wore their uniform.

Content

1. PTSD Mind 1
2. No Man Left Behind 2
3. Forced to Be a Martyr 3
4. Imprisoned 4
5. 10 x 10 5
6. Scared Mirror 7
7. Living Without Regret 9
8. Taken Captive 11
9. Bi-World 12
10. The Fiend Chasing the Demon in the Glass Pipe ... 14
11. Gold 16
12. Crippling 18
13. My Brother's Keeper 19
14. The Puppet Master 21
15. On That Cross 23
16. For A Blind Moment 24
17. In The Box 25
18. The Beast 27
19. Words 29
20. My Gethsemane 31
21. My Name is Crack 33
22. Baby 35
23. Lured into Darkness 37
24. Hands Dipped in Blood 39
25. Oblivious 41
26. Warrior Without a Leader 43
27. 3 Minutes 45

28. Suddenly	47
29. Hardships of the Homeless	49
30. Hatred	50
31. The Search for Truth	51
32. For Pennies on a Dollar	53
33. Limelight	55
34. When Life Fails	57
35. Compromise	59
36. Stealth Words	61
37. -ed	63
38. Healing of a Nation	64
39. On Synthetics	66
40. Self-Imposed	68
41. This is My Intercession	70
42. After the Sun Rises	72
43. Implosion vs. Explosion	74
44. In Thought	76
45. Lost Memories	77
46. Lurking in Shadows	79
47. Not Born	81
48. Other People's Eyes	83
49. Portrait of a Tattoo in Ink	84
50. Rage	86
51. These Walls	88
52. Violent Children	89
53. Wild Child	91
54. Without Tomorrow	93
55. Past/Present/Future	95
56. Too Familiar	97
57. Poeticification	99
58. Hypocrite	101
59. Sinocrite	103
60. Saintocrite	105
61. Lower Than Low	107
62. Oppressor Oppressed	110

63. In Time	112
64. On the Verge Of	113
65. Crisis	115
66. I Will Face	117
67. My Heart	119
68. Hell	121
69. Better or Bitter?	122
70. I've Been Through	124
71. Don't Hit My Mama!	125
72. In Prison	127
73. In There	129
74. Perpetrate	131
75. The Chameleon Syndrome	133
76. The Fight	135
77. This Brown Skin	137
78. Tranquility	139
79. U Left Too Soon	140
80. Wanted	142
81. Hypocrisy	144
82. After the Dance	146
83. Brother Down	148
84. Combat Ready	150
85. Fashioned by the Hand of God	152
86. I Refuse!	154
87. Nothing to Fear	155
88. There's No	156
89. The Lies of Men	158
90. Judas Heart	160
91. The Power of Consent	162
92. A Sense of Loss	164
93. Left to Myself	166
94. Alternate Reality	168
95. Lonely Walk	169
96. When Facing a Mountain	170
97. No Other Recourse	172

98. In the Depths	173
99. Recidivism	174
100. Souls Passing Over	175
101. Triggers	177

PTSD Mind

My mind runs from yesterday's memories of trauma unknown.
My exposure to human crisis set me on the edge.
Nothing is as it used to be.

At times, I feel caged within this cyclical process of human suffering,
repeating moments I can't escape.

I live in a constant state of emergency.

My mind is thrown back and forth from reality to unreality,
because rage buries these painful memories,
and I seek help from those who can bring my unreality
back to normality where I can find peace of mind.

In my personal asylum, nightmares replace dreams,
fear replaces strength, despair replaces hope,
but I will hold on and cope with whatever comes my way,
because I am a survivor.

No Man Left Behind

In wartime, the motto is "No Man Left Behind."
A dying comrade is never abandoned on the battlefield.

There is no stronger love than the love created
between two men who swore an oath to defend each other
at the cost of their own lives, no greater oath
than the promise to defend one's country.

To risk your life by putting yourself in harm's way
is called selflessness.
It is a sign of bravery, courage, and honor.

This philosophy should apply not only to the military,
but to everyday civilian life.
Our perceptions of one another would change
if only we learned "I can't live without you,
and you can't live without my help."

In times of crisis, it takes a community,
bound by honor and loyalty,
to overcome any unexpected conflict.

If we stay ready, we no longer have to get ready.

Forced to Be a Martyr

Too much is at stake - the Savior couldn't wait,
as the sands of time seeped through the hourglass,
as our lives bled into eternal time.
The Creator never intended mankind
to lose all hope of redemption,
but our enemies were scheming against us,
so He, Christ, was forced to be a martyr,
to free the bound souls,
lost over what was perceived as fool's gold
sold to humanity.
Now the people scream
because they believed the enemy's lies.
The enemy hated humanity
from the beginning,
and because of our disobedience,
the Savior was forced to be a martyr,
giving his own life
to make things right.

Imprisoned

I am imprisoned by trauma.
I am a product of conflict.

I believed it was my duty
to serve and protect
the freedoms I love most.

I was ready and willing to fight
until my last breath.

I've seen people, shackled
by the burdens of men,
who cared not for their own survival.
Whether they lived or died
meant nothing to them,
so long as they could rule with an iron fist.

I am imprisoned by trauma,
a product of conflict.

No longer will I sit idle,
like the proverbial fog
hovering above a pot of water
while the heat is turned up,
dying slowly.

10 x 10

I just moved into a 10x10 room.
Somehow, I stuffed everything I own
into this little home,
but my surroundings feel so estranged,
and my life feels rearranged.
I'm feeling the pain
of being tossed aside,
a part of me has died a thousand deaths,
and I can't even collect death benefits -
I need to make adjustments,
but my beliefs won't bend,
and I'm trapped in this maze,
fading into a world with no end.
Still, a 10x10 is better than
living on the dark and lonely streets
with nothing to eat, trying to survive,
trying to forget how far you've fallen
from grace.
In my case, I'm just trying to trace
from where I fell
and why my life went to hell,
no money for bail,
and all I could do was yell.
Maybe someone will have mercy on me,
drop a few dimes,
but it's so rough

trying to tough it out
while I wait for blessings to fall from the sky,
begging the Heavens, "Oh me oh my, may I please
have a piece of the pie before I die?"
It's been quite an experience
living within a 10x10 room,
and one day, when I leave,
I hope I'm ready to cope with something bigger
than a 10x10, but until then,
I'm gonna work with it until I can kick it
with the big ballers.

Scared Mirror

As I gaze upon the window
that reflects the image of who I am,
it shows me a misnomer
of my true self.

I've struggled with distorted perceptions
of the other self
while searching for my own greatness,

I've discovered my altered ego
while pondering my future.

I've discussed the multi-dimensional complexities
of the inner and outer selves
with me, myself, and I,
and we came to the conclusion
that the nomenclature of my existence
must be birthed from within the circle
of my confidants.

The mass destruction caused
by others' words
have temporarily stifled my progress to glory,
but I will not be defeated.

Though I've been bruised, misused,
ostracized and scandalized,
I rise above my burdens,
and my brokenness will be the formation
of the real me
as I rise from the ashes of obscurity.

Living Without Regret

As I look back upon my life,
I see so many mistakes,
and sometimes I wish I could go back in time
and change my mind,
but it is what it is.

I was young then,
very young,
and I did not understand life's plan,
but now that I am a man,
I see things more clearly.

If I had known about life's many tricks
and traps,
I wouldn't have had to fight so hard
just to stay above water.

I lost so much time,
trying to keep my head above water,
but now there's no time to lose.
As the clock tick tocks,
I must not waste any time reliving the past,
chasing a make-believe
that was never conceived.

Life has taught me
to learn from the past,
to cherish the present,
and to live without regret.

Taken Captive

Who knows why certain circumstances arise in our lives?
Daily, we see anomalies preventing humanity
from reaching their true potential.

Those of us on the forefront of liberty
must fight, advocate, and direct hope
towards self-sufficiency,
building the body, soul, and spirit.

We who have insight
must become an integral part of their
journey towards the Promised Land
of autonomy,
helping those who struggle,
guiding them,
showing them how to take control
of their own destinies.

I would be remiss
if I spoke not of victory,
of rising above the fog of uncertainty,
of walking through the unobtainable fortresses
to a place called Freedom,
where you're no longer wrestling with failure,
but walking in triumph.

Bi-World

Life is a rollercoaster
for those torn between sanity and insanity.
The mind ebbs and flows,
which may be perceived as torment,
hallucinations,
episodes of madness.

To live in a bi-world can be confusing
as one tries to find an anchor of hope
to cope with the light and dark sides,

but deep within every soul
lies the will to rise
and challenge every force of oppression
that seeks to imprison the ones
with free will.

Life is filled with uncertainties
and mysteries,
but one who is willing to combat every force
will triumph.
There is no greater power than friendship,
and we must trust the counsel
of those who have proven themselves indispensable.

It's difficult to be trapped on life's roller coaster.
You go up one day and down the next,
never able to maintain a firm grip on stability,
struggling to live inside one reality
while dealing with insanity.

The Fiend Chasing the Demon in the Glass Pipe

Some say it Ain't right
to die for a puff of smoke
from a glass pipe,
but it feels right.
One puff, now you're hooked
on the cookie crook
because it looks good to cook that rock.
It'll make you feel like a god,
but in reality, it's an evil demon.

It knows your weakness,
and its mission is to bring pain
into another life.
Tonight will be like so many other nights,
so many sistas and brothas bound
because they're fiends chasing the demon
in the glass pipe.

One puff just Ain't enough,
keep chasing that dream,
it's no more than a scheme
to steal your soul.
You'll be dragged down the path of the lost
once you take a puff of that stuff,
you give up your right to choose,
you became a fool, sold your soul,

and you cry out for help
because this demon is too strong to fight alone.

Just know there is hope for those who fall,
a fifty-fifty chance,
maybe you'll win, maybe you won't,
so smokers beware
of becoming the fiend
chasing the demon
in the glass pipe.

Gold

Like gold, I rise to the top,
too powerful to be stopped.
I've been trapped on the bottom
waiting for the right time
to float like a boat.

The dross can no longer weigh me down
with steel bars forged from past crimes.
I no longer wear a frown,
my struggles have been my making,
and I'm still in the process
of breaking free from the chains of the past.

My power surges like a burst of new energy.
I can see light at the end of this tunnel -
no longer hanging out with the enemies
who claimed to be friends,
promising they'd stick with me to the very end,

but things change, people change too,
and now I'm on a fast track to success,
leaving my old life behind.

I see golden dust sparkling
in my own eyes.
I am no longer living that old life.

Today, I walk in freedom.
Like gold, I have reached my destiny.

Crippling

They spoke of death when I was an adolescent,
without realizing they were unleashing a curse
to purge my power,
attempting to incarcerate my potential
of freeing others encaged by their own dark nature.

I've gone through that stage of probability,
pressing to reach the zenith of my destiny.
Their words were crippling,
and they tried to alter great change
for the good.

Their words inundated my environment
with false illusions to keep me from my calling,
words laced with deception,
disguised as transparent agents of love.

Over time, I realized darkness and light don't mix,
and I refused to accept their preconceived plan
for my life.

I rose from obscurity,
learned how to combat death
with life.
I was able to cut the weeds
that had been planted in the fertile grounds
of my mind, and I became the victor
who spoke my own destiny.

My Brother's Keeper

My brother's keeper
has a mouth full of rocks.
He ran for years,
caused so much heartache
and so many tears.

Never would I have thought
he would renege upon his word
and betray my trust.
At times, I wanted to yield
because I was mad as hell,
and I wished him in jail.
He should have to pay a fine
for deceiving and misleading us.

He was callous, bold, and cold as a thief
selling fool's gold.
How could he have done this,
when he claimed to serve the same God that we did?
I won't be denied the money he stole from me,
but the truth Ain't been exposed.

All souls belong to God, and I asked Him
why people take advantage of others,
why they steal from their brothers.

I must not fill my soul with bitterness.
I must pray and not stray from my faith.

Jesus knows mercy -
for greater love hath no man than he
who would lay his life down for a friend,

and Christ is my brother's keeper,
He who forsakes no one.
Jesus took away all my blues
and left me with sweet sunshine,
I even watched Him heal the blind,

and He never lets me stumble
or crumble under pressure
when things get too hot to handle.

He'll be right there,
and I swear to tell the truth,
the whole truth,
and nothing but the truth,
so help me God,
for Jesus truly is my brother's keeper.

The Puppet Master

The puppet master controls the flow of their lyrics
through manipulation.
The people sold their souls for fame,
perceived financial gain,
and a gold chain,
but they are nothing more than slaves
with a little more change,
and the price will be their lives
as they strive
forward with the notion that they're rich,
but they have not kept the cost in mind,
they went blind.
They're dying to be known
but they'll just become
cold tombstones.

They wrote their names in blood
on the dotted line
without reading the fine print,
and the puppet master moves to seal the deal
while stealthily seducing their will
to kill all resistance to the master plan,
and they are incapable of cutting the strings
strangling their dreams,
too caught up in the lies,

leading themselves down a path of darkness,
eradicating the light
as well as the desire
to fight for their own lives.

On That Cross

I did not know there was a man
dying on that cross for me:
beaten, bruised,
and accused of a crime
that was never proven
in a court of law.

He was beaten beyond recognition,
and it was now my mission
to find the truth.

People say that the truth
shall set you free,
but in His case,
although he was an innocent man,
they would devise an evil plan
to mislead those at hand.

Today, I understand the power of sin,
and the affliction of Him
as I walk through the valley
of the shadow of death.

Born upon the banner of death,
I feel it trying to squeeze what life I have left,
trying to finish its mission
without regret,
but I refuse to die
without a fight.

For A Blind Moment

For a blind moment,
I could not see that God had a purpose for me.
It has been written
that when the enemy rushes in
like a flood
that the spirit of the Lord
stands against evil
and defeats him at his own game,
and there Ain't no shame,
because Jesus took all the blame
when he was laid upon that cross.

The Lord shows himself to be strong
to those whose hearts are loyal only to him,
and sometimes for a blind moment,
we all get sidetracked, misdirected
on the tracks to destiny,
but with faith in Jesus Christ,
you know you're right -
He shall direct your steps,
so don't contemplate, just submit,
for it is said that in Christ, we shall know abundance
every day and night,
and when the enemy comes for you,
he shall flee
when he sees God at your side,
and no longer will you be blind.

In The Box

In this box,
I am surrounded by
impenetrable walls.
As I try to push forward,
I feel invisible barriers
blocking every step
I try to take,
but there is something
within the depths of my soul
that says *No*.
It says, "You will rise above this struggle,"
and I know I will.

I will climb out from this box,
I will continue chasing my dream,
I will watch my vision
explode before me
with fervent passion.

My love is stronger than this difficulty,
my dreams greater
than any earthly obstacle,
and my determination
is more potent than any enemy.

Being trapped in this box
has only strengthened my power,
and I will one day climb out
and enter this strange new world
called Freedom.

The Beast

The beast within me is a rebel
trying to sin against its master.
All it knows is disaster,
incarcerated by the flesh,
trying to test the outer man
to see if he can withstand the pressure.

The beast cries out "Just let me bless ya"
with a little coke so I can get blowed,
so I can float on down the river,
because my ship has just come in,
and I don't need friends.

I'm about to get buck wild child,
so jump in line
if you want to do some time.
I'll treat you like a hound.
I'm a pure animal,
bow wow, meow meow,
and sometimes I'm a clown,
but I want you to be my friend,
so when you need a favor,
you don't have to call your Savior.
I'm ready to get down

and do my thing,
if you know what I mean,
because I Ain't clean, I'm real nasty,
and that's just the way
the world likes me.

I was born a beast,
and I am destined to die
a beast.

Words

Your words prevented my darkness
from destroying me.
I was born with folly within,
but it was your unconditional love
that set me free.
You loved me
with your sweet words of mercy,
liberated me from my desolate prison,
and laid a foundation of hope
that allowed me to cope
with everyday life.
Your words became the Word.
Your words taught me
how to love you,
those words became flesh
to be tested
by life's trials and temptations.
Your words were the Logos
that became Rhema,
they created a romance
that would last a lifetime.
Now that I've been set free,
I want to tell thee
that you are my only one,
my sweet, my honey.
I want to praise you with my words,

for they are the only things I can use
to describe just how marvelous
you truly are.
You are greater than anything I've known
in this lifetime.
Your compassion is eternal,
you sheltered me
with your invisible hand,
preserving my life,
rescuing me
during my darkest hour.
At times, it's difficult to articulate
how wonderful you really are,
and I am pleased to say that I love you,
and I will proudly use my words
every day to sing
your glorious praises.

My Gethsemane

My Gethsemane
is the garden of life
in which I live,
protecting me through the many trials
and tribulations of life.
As I pray,
I feel the intense pressure
of my faith
struggling to believe
in spite of all my hardships.

The darkness feels too great,
but despite the pain,
I must answer the call to crucifixion.
I must sacrifice
so that others may benefit
from the divine power of
God Himself.

I must drink from the same cup
that Christ used,
that cup of death,
and I must trust in Him
to resurrect me from the dead.
I've already died one thousand deaths,
only to realize
that I must continue to die

in order to fulfill the purposes
of the Father.

It seems as if the more I pray,
the less my prayers are heard,
but Thy will be done, not mine,
and Lord, as I struggle to pray
in the garden of my Gethsemane,
I finally realize
that my sole purpose
is to fulfill the destiny
You created for me.

My Name is Crack

My name is crack,
and baby, I'll make you act a fool.
Mess with me
and you'll lose everything,
but if you want to play, you've got to pay,
and there's not a day
that goes by where somebody Ain't down with me.
I'll bring you to your knees,
make you beg "Pretty please."
I'll be your God,
and you'll worship me,
because I'll feed you a substance
that will keep you runnin'
here, there, and everywhere,
like a puppet on a string
with a hook in your nose
and a noose around your neck.
I'm like a controller,
a big-time roller,
and all the men, all the ladies
know I'll drive them crazy.
Just take one hit from this pipe,
and you won't be able to get me
off your mind.
I'll get you so high
you won't have a clue what to do,

so don't call anyone else but me,
because I'm available twenty-four-seven.
Whenever you need a fix,
come on over and get some.
I'll tell you again:
crack is my name,
and gettin' folks hooked
is my game,
sweet as candied yams,
come taste how sweet and I can be,
and never forget, baby,
that your first taste
is free.

Baby

He's just a small baby boy
sucking on a pacifier,
but one day, he will be a man.
He needs to be cared for
by the right hands,
not destroyed before he has a chance to grow.

In this world,
neglect is at an all-time high -
babies are birthed
by the thousands
and thrust into a cold, callous life
where there's no room to groom
a boy into a man.

He's still an infant,
he hasn't learned of society's dark ways
yet.
He will become a product
of his teachings, his training, his environment,
and if he does off the deep end,
people will whisper behind his back
that he used to be "such a cute little baby."

As parents, we never know who we're raising
until that child grows
beyond our control.

Every child is born a baby,
but tell me, which kind of baby
do you wish to create,
a healer,
or a killer?

Lured into Darkness

Though he understood the light, he was drawn in
by the darkness,
taking a risk on the possibility
of *maybe*.
Something tickled his curiosity
by moving beyond the boundaries of safety,
and he knew the journey
he was set to embark upon
would cost him everything.

He had his eyes on the prize,
and there was no price too large
to pay.
Hooked by the gambler's spirit,
he proceeded to carry out
the suicide mission
he signed up for --
the thrill of conquer
and the promise of adrenaline
was too tempting to refuse.

"Life is filled with many different doors,"
he told himself,
"and we must allow those doors
to open and close at will."

There is always the desire
for that elusive pot of gold
at the end of a rainbow,
only for you to reach the end
and realize you're just chasing the wind.

No man is beyond temptation.
We wrestle, not against flesh and blood,
but against rulers of darkness.
Let us pray that we are not lured into a place
where is no escape.

Hands Dipped in Blood

There stood Jesus,
hands dipped in blood,
and as He spoke,
He wiped away my sin.

I saw my name erased
from that place of judgment,
and in that moment,
I felt the burden of iniquity
lifted from my soul.

Christ was the foundation of life
in this world.
The harvest is right,
laborers are few,
and I have heard the cries of those
who have lost all hope.

His loving eyes were filled
with a fire that flickered
for all of humanity,
and in that moment, I fell to my knees,
begging,
"Lord, please send me where I am needed,"

and I heard Him whisper,
"There you shall go,"
and it was then
that I understood
that Jesus is boss, the king
and Sovereign Lord,
amen.

Oblivious

Living in a state of forgetfulness,
not perceiving the trouble
lurking on the horizon.
Things Ain't gonna get any better,
because the people won't change
their vicarious ways
as society trays
into a place of self-annihilation.

People are dying
from a lack of love for one another.
Aggression has become a passtime,
unrenewed minds killing our sons
by the dozen
with no repentance forthcoming.

Ordinary men portray themselves as God,
but the hand of judgment
has passed its verdict.
Some will live, others will die,
and it appears as if no one
can read the writing on the walls
promising that the kingdoms of men
will surely fall.

We believe we can control
a world we have no control over,
but where there is no vision,
people perish --
such is the downfall
of a nation
against its own people

Warrior Without a Leader

There are those who travel
the cold, hard streets,
trying to defend something they call life,
only to end up in a casket
behind steel doors,
with no opportunities
and no hope.

A warrior without a leader
is dangerous --
the only thing he experiences
on a constant basis is pain,
and he does not know
how to break the cycle of violence,
and this warrior cries for vengeance
against an unfair system,
all the while losing faith
in everything but himself.

A warrior without a leader
kills by instinct.
Rage flows through his veins
like a volcano about to erupt
with no prior warning.

We must stop the bloodshed.
Innocent blood cries for vengeance,
and we must all become
positive role models,
active fathers
to those with or without blood ties.

We must speak the truth.
We must keep our promises,
honor our words,
and we must tell all these lost warriors
about their Creator,
because surely, ignorance of the past
will only lead to a present day without a future.

3 Minutes

They've got 3 minutes
before a life or death situation.
There can be no underestimating
the potentiality
of someone facing their doom,
for it would soon determine their reality.

The penalty could be a life lost
without conscious thought,
or perhaps a life saved
right in the nick of time.
An act of God would do just fine.

It's been said that 105 people die
every minute.
Within the span of three minutes,
315 different dreams
have gone up in smoke,
and that Ain't no joke.

If I'm given one minute,
I can redirect someone else's attack.
If I'm given two minutes,
I can save a life,
and if I'm given three minutes,
I can stop future violence
from rocking the community.

All we need, all any of us need,
are three minutes
to bring redemption
before we face
extinction.

Suddenly

Suddenly, it seems as if today was yesterday.
Suddenly, I reflected upon a memory,
motionless
as if it were caught between time
and eternity.

Suddenly I thought *I've been here before*,
because so many things
seem familiar.

Suddenly I realized
it was not a play, but a way of life,
that the cycle of change
is the simple way
of existing between two worlds.

Suddenly I realized I would no longer hear
the voice of childhood,
for some greater power has taken dominion
over what I believed was reality.

Suddenly I realized I had no power
to change certain things,
for they were written in stone
long before I entered the world.

Suddenly, time expired into nothingness,
and I am filled with uncertainty,
asking questions, seeking answers,
filled with the need to understand
what cannot be understood.

Hardships of the Homeless

I don't want you to miss
this crisp description
of a nomad's mission,
jumping from kitchen to kitchen,
getting a daily fixin'
of food and drink.
Do you think
it's hard to be out in the yard
365 days a year,
with no shelter of your own
and no place to call home?

Dreams vanish,
acting manic,
trying to walk the planet,
but the fact remains
there Ain't enough change in Uncle Sam's pocket
to knock out this homeless problem.
The solution
to this institutional problem

is to own a piece of land,
to avoid looking in the garbage can,
because there's no future in being homeless,
so buy yourself a piece of land
and own it.

Hatred

Hatred begins in the eyes,
how they lie
about what they perceive through
blurred vision,
and once the eyes have analyzed,
the mind begins to evaluate thoughts
and intentions without mercy,
and after categorizing
what it deems worthless,
the heart begins to believe
all the lies it's been told.
The heart becomes like stone,
cold and callous
with no chance of balance,
and all the fears arise
with darkness by its side,
and we wonder why so many people needlessly die.
Hatred kills,
and it comes at the price
of not only someone else's life
but also yours.

The Search for Truth

The search for truth means
finding knowledge
from bits and pieces of information
passed down from one generation
to the next.

The search for truth is a trail
of undisclosed revelations
kept from those who desperately need answers,
where one asks questions that illuminate the mind
and reveal pain
that may last a lifetime.

The truth, the whole truth,
and nothing but the truth
can help you find peace of mind
and allow you to close the door
on disappointment, frustration,
and confusion.

The moment of truth
may not ever come,
but at least you made an effort
to locate the missing pieces of history.

We're all affected by unspoken truths
that transform our lives,
both for better and for worse,

but overall,
we tend to bounce back quickly
from tragedy and despair.

Life is filled with many enigmas,
riddles,
and puzzling detours
from the reality we call our lives,
but those lives go on,
and so does our quest to know the unknown.

Maybe it would be better
if we just left well enough alone
and accepted that which we do not know.

Every person has something in their life
that raises questions,
arouses suspicion,
and maybe our only choice
is to keep pushing forward
towards a bright future
and leave whatever happened in the past
safely in the past.

For Pennies on a Dollar

A life is taken
for a little bit of nothing,
and to the money hunters,
life doesn't really mean anything,
except that which creates false dreams.

Young men fantasize about shiny cars,
fine jewelry, fancy clothes,
and beautiful women,
but those dreams are short-lived,
because there was a time
when they used to snort that white stuff,
and the price was too high,
so they found a way to turn that white stuff"
into a rock that brought the price down
like cheap stock
during a bad day on Wall Street.

In order to keep demand high,
they changed the way the game was played,
keeping the addicts at bay,
selling poison to one another.

It could be urban, suburban,
and rural, too,
but the greatest danger is when

they live right next to you
when you don't have a clue.

For pennies on a dollar,
they'll fight and kill
over things that seem so unreal,
until they finally pull back the sheets,
take a peep,
and laugh as they realize
that you are their next victim.

Limelight

Standing in the limelight brings much praise
to the one being recognized
for their great contribution to society.
The limelight is a place
where you're exposed to the world,
so that they may be privileged enough
to view your gifts and talents.

In the limelight,
people will love you
as long as you fit their perception
of perfection,
but they have little tolerance for failure
and disappointment.

We want to believe that those
standing in the limelight
are superhuman,
and when our humanity reveals itself,
those in the limelight
are deemed unworthy of adoration.

Though we understand frailty
to a degree,
we tend to forget that everyone is flawed.

The limelight is like a double-edged blade
cutting both ways,
and when we reach that level of fame,
we will discover our weaknesses
and flaws there in the limelight.

When Life Fails

There are no guarantees in life,
only struggles.

I often ask myself
if I am in the right place at the right time,
because everything in life is about timing.
I'm seeking answers
that have escaped me,
and at times, the answers I receive
don't make sense.

The seasons of life are unpredictable,
and one must always be prepared
to face unseen obstacles
that will hinder your progress.

When life fails, you must try
again and again until you succeed
in your quest to achieve your dreams.
Life has a funny way
of handing you a task that seems impossible
as a way to test your fighting spirit.

I often wonder why
dreams must be birthed from pain.
Nothing in life comes easily,

but any struggle is worth the price
so long as you are willing
to pay it.

When life fails,
when you have no answers
for the dilemma you're facing,
you must stand firm,
and your true power will emerge.

All things manifest in time.
The hardest lesson to learn
is that you never know what's waiting for you
around the corner,
even when you think you know,
and you must be ready
to tackle life's many obstacles
with every ounce of courage
and conviction,
and when you do that,
you will see there are two sides to life,
positive and negative,
and both are needed
to mold us
into the human beings
we are destined to become.

Compromise

I used to compromise my beliefs
just to get some relief,
and at times, my desires
were like flaming trees
burning out of control.

Never do anything that doesn't
correlate to your dreams
or push you forward on your journey,
or else your dreams
may turn into schemes,
and schemes turn into nightmares,
so be wary of your dark side.

Don't lose your passion.

Don't sacrifice your identity.

Don't let yourself be transformed
into someone you don't recognize,
or else you might feel like a failure
before you even dare
to reach for your dreams.

Stay on track,
and everything will work out.

Don't compromise who you are,
and you won't be surprised
when you finally meet
your true self.

Stealth Words

A stealth word
is something I've heard of,
a word that doesn't sound quite right,
trying to slip under the radar.

You say things
because you're trying to make a point,
but it's to no avail,
because you create hell.
There's a hidden code within your words,
accusing me of doing something
I would never do,

but I am free to be me,
and I won't let someone else's words
trap me.
You see, I believe that I'm not bound
by any sound,
because I've been around too long
and have found my strength
within.

Your stealth words were used
to destroy the confidence
of your perceived enemy,
but you were not aware
that I picked up on your secret codes,

and then your words became
nothing
but hollow noises
echoing through the airways.

-ed

We have been subjugated, relegated, implicated,
castigated, ejaculated,
bastardgated, objectigated, objectivated, emasculated,
separated,
segregated,
tolerated, frustrated, assassinated, irritated,
underrated, underestimated, adulterated,
infiltrated, incinerated, unappreciated.

We are unsatisfied,
unpasteurized, euthanized,
denied, falsified, unrealized, unrecognized,
vilified, nullified, demonized,
pillarized, unmemorized,
and all the other ed's.

Now it's time for a change,
and that change
can only begin
with us.

Healing of a Nation

The people of our nation have been affected
by the loss of loved ones.
Many tears have fallen from their eyes
morning, noon, and night.

Loss brings pain, but in their pain,
the God of Heaven heals them,
using His healing hands to once again
bring wholeness to a broken nation.

Our Lord is the God
of both the living and the dead.
Though the people have suffered loss,
God will never fade away,
and He will always be with you
until the very end.

Life is filled with many unexpected situations
that bring anguish and disappointment,
but he who follows God lives forever,
and those who are called
according to His perfect will
are sometimes lost forever
to the streets we walk every day,

so we must pray that God will stop
all the senseless violence in the world,
and as we pray, we give God permission
to complete his perfect will,
so that we may live to face another day.

On Synthetics

I see the effects of synthetics on your face,
I see how it has distorted your vision,
and through someone else's mission,
you have become a byproduct
of permission,
led by the will of another
to control your intentions
without any remission.

Your only desire
is to fulfill their status quo.
Your submission is killing
your will to love,
you're losing your mind,
you're not even fighting,
you just keep giving to a cause
that will lead to your downfall.

When you cry,
no one will come to your rescue,
and as I look around,
I see so many others
who have pledged their lives
to a cause not their own,
wondering why they never felt at home.

It's the synthetics that tricked them
in the first place,

and now they have nowhere
to rest their heads
except an open grave.

They thought they were brave enough
to take the dare,
and now they're falling through the abyss,
trapped in the heat of their first kiss
with the myth of synthetics.

They have no power to resist,
and they wish for the control
they once had,
shackled by what they believed
would be the ultimate thrill,
when the reality is
it was nothing more than a pill,
a powder,
a substance to smoke, snort,
or swallow,
and when it's all said and done,
you will be the one
living in a cage
of your own surprise,
playing around with strychnine,
playing the game of death.

Graves are full of those
that walked blind,
those who lost their minds,
all because they were on synthetics,
falling through a trapdoor
that leads to
nowhere.

Self-Imposed

As I look over my life, I see some struggles
were self-imposed.
Time after time, I thought I made
the right decision,
only to end up on the wrong
mission.
I didn't seek the right information
that would have brought reformation,
rather than incarceration.

How could I have ended up
making so many poor choices
that brought no joy?

I'm retracing my steps,
looking for the wrong turn I made
way back then.
I'm trying to get back on track
to my ultimate destination,
but I need help to change my circumstances.

It's a blessing
when life is going so smoothly,
it causes a brother to move
at the speed of light,
only to find that my flight was cancelled,

but I'm still hoping
to find my way out of this maze
while I continue to dream
about being on top
instead of being trapped, self-imposed
at the bottom.

This is My Intercession

Lord, you've built a wall of protection
around me,
and you said you would spare the soul
of any man willing to serve you,
for you are not willing to lose anyone
after the price you paid on Calvary
two thousand years ago,
so I fall upon my knees
and pray.

I'm willing to do whatever it takes,
so that the lost souls
may escape your wrath.
This is my intercession.

God, I ask that you would have mercy
upon me that I might be able to pray
for those who are lost
and loving lives of darkness.

I recognize that some things
are not pleasing to thee,
and I raise my voice for you, oh God,
that you might hear the plea
of my supplication
as I pray for the restoration of a nation
that is lost.

This will be my sacrifice,
my price to pay,
until you set all men free.

This is my intercession.

After the Sun Rises

After the sun rises, life changes,
and with those changes
come feelings of love and loss,
and we remember why it hurts so much
to lose someone we loved —
that departed soul left behind a legacy
of love and affection
that causes us to love them more.

After the sun rises, we begin to reflect
upon the times and moments
which are so dear to our hearts,
and at times, there are no words
to express how we feel.
The time we have left
is meant for loving, giving,
and sharing our most prices possessions:
our memories.

After the sun rises, joy shall wash upon us
like a blanket of divine protection,
giving us the strength to walk the path
stretching before us,
even if we don't understand the reason
why.

We must live each day like it's our last.
We must give love that is pure, and unconditional.

We must breathe life into those who are broken,
and lift those who need a helping hand.

We must love the unlovable,
show patience to those who test
our beliefs.

Love is the greatest power on earth,
and we must use it to improve the lives
of others,
to create a better world for all.

After the sun rises, the moon sets,
and we shall understand this thing
called life,
as the cycle of giving and taking
continues,

and as long as we are on this earth,
we must let our love be seen,
our truths revealed,
and our visions fulfilled.

Implosion vs. Explosion

The implosion of emotions
creates a variety of mental issues
that destroy the soul from the inside,
where unleashed anger resides.

Tempers are at an all-time high
as the people feel self-hatred
without understanding why —
they are tormented by inner struggles,
crying from within,
searching for a friend they can trust.

Explosion is a different kind of game,
switching from inward to outward shame,
unable to tame
the beast within
as it breaks loose
and begins to sin.

Explosion is a monster that can't be controlled; it goes
with the flow of circumstances.
It doesn't need facts, it acts
impulsively,
because it has full liberty
to do as it pleases.

Explosion reveals its true colors,
it will assault a sister, or even a brother.
It knows no boundaries, feels no shame,
and has no goal but to dominate.

Implosion is the pain within,
while explosion is that pain
expressed without.

In Thought

I loved in thought.
I hated in thought.
I blessed in thought.
I cursed in thought.
I told the truth in thought.
I lied in thought.
I've killed in thought.
I've saved lives in thought.
I destroyed in thought,
I lived in thought.
I died in thought.
I see in thought,
and I know now, in thought.

Lost Memories

I lost my memories of yesterday day's folly;
I can't quite remember how I danced
to the beat of darkness, unrepentant,
and I can't find a way
to return to the light.

I'm fighting a battle unseen
through my reality, my dreams.
How can I achieve victory?
I lost my mind
for a spell of a time,
playing with the devil's fiddle
trying to decipher life's many riddles.

Living like there's no tomorrow,
feeling numb, full of sorrow,
tryin' to borrow a little time
before it's my turn to transpire
from this empire,
but I rose to the occasion
before the break of day,
only to fade deeper into the abyss,
going totally insane.

Amnesia seems to be my passtime,
but my retention is at an all-time high,
until I begin to fly

beyond the stars in my mind
living on cloud nine,
so I will try to take my time
and tell it like it is.

This is the crazy phase people go through
when they act out of the ordinary.

Contrary to the truth,
these people think they're okay
and it kind of seems like we all think we're okay,
doesn't it,
until someone brings to our attention
that we aren't all there,
and it seems fair
to receive what you better believe
you've got comin' to you
for the possibility of recovering
all these lost memories.

Lurking in Shadows

They lurk in shadows, waiting for night,
not wanting to be exposed
as the beast within their souls
is ready to feast upon young, innocent children
with hypocritical pretense.
Their main agenda
is to annihilate the weak
before the weak become strong enough
to defend themselves.

This type of shadow walker
lives in every city, and every country,
wandering endlessly through society,
sacrificing others.
Their thirst is in the folly of evil intent,
and they conceal their dark side
with fluorescent lights
so bright they appear as angels of the night.

Their ring of terror begins
while children are small
and not fully developed enough
to tell it all,
but we must reveal the hand
of the enemy
before our children's memories
are stained with shame and inequity.

We must fight for those
who cannot defend themselves.
We must shine our healing light upon the world,
for the ones who lurk in the shadows are bold,
but only when those lights burn out.

Not Born

Men are not born beaters of women,
but somewhere along the way,
they experienced or witnessed trauma,
which made them develop a habit
unconsciously
that triggers violence against women.

No little boy walks around bragging:
"I'm going to beat women when I grow up."
For the most part,
he probably won't grow old enough
to accomplish such a dastardly deed.

When children witness violence
at a young age,
seeds are planted,
and after a while, it becomes commonplace
to slap the one he claims to love.

Respect is nowhere to be found,
and without giving it a second thought,
he has done the unthinkable,
and she has already hit the ground.

Behaviors can be changed,
as long as he is willing to repent his hateful ways.
A baby boy is not meant
to hate the one who gave him life.

Children imitate their parents,
and we must all be careful
not to create monsters.
Parents must be responsible, and held accountable,
not only to our children but to society as a whole.

Other People's Eyes

As I listened to someone else's words,
I was able to capture some visuals
that formed my perception,
as my mind was able to draw a picture
of someone my eyes have never beheld,
and as my mind deciphered an image,
it created a portrait of someone beautiful.

In that moment, love was pure, unreserved,
and I had no time to make a preconceived judgment
based on imperfection and expectations.

I had no time to contemplate
the pros and cons of a possible love affair,
but my intuition was heightened,
and I was way beyond the point of moving
back and forth between the choice to give someone
a lifetime of love or not.

It was through someone else's eyes
that I made the decision to love
and be loved, and now I've developed this ability to love
not only through touch, feelings,
and emotions, but through the revelations hidden within
other people's eyes.

Portrait of a Tattoo in Ink

His beginning was great,
as the history of his life
was tattooed by the pen of a skilled writer.
His trials and tribulations
granted him the ability to make choices
that would either lead to his demise
or lead him to a Promised Land of hope.

The sketch on his body,
the "Angel of Death,"
was born from the imagination
of a traumatized individual,
bruised by a society displaying its beliefs
into the dark ink in his skin,
serving as a reminder
to remember his legacy, always.
His long history of neglect
as a child led to a life of complication and trepidation.

Tattoos are biographies
journaled on a soul's outer shell,
hidden messages
understood only by those who share
similar experiences.

Some tattoos are crossword puzzles,
keeping their true meanings hidden,
but once that revelation has been revealed,
only then will we begin to understood
the portrait of the tattoo in ink.

Rage

His rage came out through his words.
He was angry,
because at times, life seemed unfair,
and he tried to do the right thing,
but it often felt as if God
was nowhere to be found.

He complained about losing faith
in the One he thought was his Provider,
until he realized the only one he could trust
was himself.

He tried to provide for his sons,
and I told him I understood,
hoping it would ease his pain,
but it seemed like nothing I said
comforted him during his moments of despair.

I had no solutions,
other than to speak positively
in the face of his negativity,
and I felt his sorrows flowing through my own veins.
I sensed the hope draining from his heart,
as doubt saturated his thoughts
like a plague waiting to convert the living
to the dead.

His eyes became unrecognizable,
and my heart filled with sorrow,
because I knew he would no longer follow
the beliefs he used to have —
he was too busy seeking a painkiller
to suppress the thoughts of going
one more day without a miracle.

His light grew dimmer and dimmer,
until eventually he lost his way
and could no longer remember
that hope was the key to liberation.

These Walls

Behind these walls lies a living hell
I can't seem to escape.
Night after night, I repeat this cycle
of relentless torment,
trapped within this awful space.

I feel violent displays
that shatter my tranquility
during my season of rest.
I'm fighting an endless battle
against the circumstances.

So far, I haven't found a solution.
How does a man fight an enemy he cannot see?

How can a man hope for victory
without truth?

I have not found answer to my dilemma
yet, but my soul continues to search the universe
for a cure to my life lived in limbo.

I'm seeking a higher power
greater than all the powers
I have ever known.

I am seeking relief
from the battle I continue to fight,
trapped within these walls.

Violent Children

Violent children become violent
because their role models
perpetually displayed acts of aggression
against one another
while the children watched in horror.

Confused, paralyzed by fear,
these children internalized the pain
and the shame, guilty by association,
incarcerated by their torment
with no ability to escape.

They're living their lives,
unable to find closure,
innocent victims of rage.

Violent children
are the children of other violent children --
parents pass down the legacy
of destruction,
generation after generation,
unable to stop the cycle,
but we must break the ties
that bind this generation of broken children.

We must free them from bondage.

We must not only speak, but
take action to increase awareness
of their hidden pain in order to find a way to heal
and protect those who cannot defend themselves.

If not, we will surely become
a more violent society.

Wild Child

Our children are running wild,
and they seem to have lost
all sense of control
as they roll down the hill of destruction,
wondering if anyone really cares
about them.

Why are our children so mad?
Left alone, they will wreck havoc
on society,
impacting the world for all
future generations.

Every wild child needs love
and firm instruction
from those with knowledge.
Our children are caught in bondage,
because of a lack of care and oversight,
while they are staying up all night,
instructed by the TV and deadly websites.

Nowhere to be found are fathers,
mothers, sisters or brothers,
to relay vital information
that would bring reformation
to a nation of children
dying from a lack of education.

The world is inflated with ignorance.
There is a great failure in our families,
in our homes while our children roam the streets,
trying to find something to eat.

They wish to rise from poverty,
but they end up being pimped
for free labor by an unsympathetic system.

Our children have lost their focus,
because there is no divine order
to guide them through the darkest nights.

Receiving a proper education
is the key
to leveling the playing field
and helping our children
achieve success.

Without Tomorrow

Without tomorrow,
my life would be filled with sorrow,
because you're the life
that reflects the light of day,
helping me find my way
back to grace.

I wish to be free
from things that would bind me,
but I can see your hand of mercy
reaching for me when I fall.

All is fair in love and war,
but in this life,
we must be aware that others care
about our state of mind.

We must pause
and take the time to meditate
before we go buck wild
and become a foster child,
but in reality,
all we want is to be free.

Without tomorrow, we would all lose sight
and continue to fight
about things that don't really matter.
We seem continuously frustrated
by our circumstances,
yet we continue searching
for something greater than ourselves.

We should give thanks
for every little blessing.
After all your trials, remember this
one thing:
renewing your mind
gives you so much more time
to live your life.
Remember:
you can be happy
today.

Past/Present/Future

The past has already happened —
a memory that lingers
in the back of your mind,
a constant reminder
that it used to exist.

The present is the here and now,
which sounds up-to-date,
in-the-moment, and in-your-face,
and there's no denying that it's here.
There's no denying
that you need to face your problems,
and I know you wish you could make those problems
disappear, you'd rather go with the flow,
but you can't get rid of your problems
by ignoring them.

The future hasn't happened yet —
it's the brighter day
you're making plans for,
and it seems so far away,
but hey, it Ain't so bad,
don't feel so bad,
at least you can still plan —
you can make adjustments, if need be.

Learn from the past,
and you'll last a long time,
if you don't mind.
Learn from today,
because your goal is the future,
and in the future,
don't let the past or present
get you down.

Just keep your eyes on the prize.
Live long,
be strong,
because if there's one thing I know,
it's that a brighter day
will always come.

Too Familiar

Some people think they know you
after one casual conversation,
and over time, they think they know
exactly what you want,
but in reality, they only assume they know,
and they begin to give you
what they think you want,
but truth be told, they have become
all too familiar with you.

Familiarity is an unhealthy way of saying,
"I got this" in layman's terms,
but you are missing the mark.

Sometimes you tell people what you want,
and I believe they mean well,
but they can't seem to break the cycle
of being too familiar.

Nothing is more disheartening than for people
to hear what you ask from them
and then do the complete opposite.
Mind boggling
that you would ask for one thing
and get something else.

To assume anything
without knowing all the details
is a recipe for disaster —
I guess that's why
we find out later, rather than sooner,
that our Dr. Jekyll
turns out to be a Mr. Hyde.

Getting to know people
takes a long time,
and we must not assume
that we know anything about them
until we have taken the time
to ask questions.

Authentic truth only reveals itself
through the transparency
of a person's heart,
and once someone's heart is
transparent,
then and only then
will we be able to learn
the truth about that person.

Poeticification

Poeticification is the process
of turning difficult situations
into abstract revelations,
moving beyond the obstacles and pitfalls
we all struggle against,

because we're not bound by every
negative sound,
nor the mountains
that seem to look like walls,
but we push through the darkness.

We rise, thanks to wisdom and knowledge.
We merge from obscurity, finding hope
to help us cope with our negative thoughts.
We find strength in the counsel
and helping hands
of our fellow man.

Sometimes people just need to talk
about their ailments
in order to remove all contaminants.

Sometimes our minds are poisoned over time
through abuse and misuse.

Sometimes people die
with none of their questions answered.

We must hear the cries of their suffering
and try to make a difference in their lives
while we still can.

It is through poetification
that I've won my many battles
with the dark side,
and now I can hear their cries for help.
I have allowed my past experiences
to act as a guiding light
for those who are lost.

If we unite to fight
the unseen enemies of the mind,
we can finally remove our blinders,
so that we can finally see
where the struggles are
and bless those individuals
hoping for a better day.

Let each and every day
serve as a new beginning
for those who have found a new way
to say, "I shall overcome."

There is no obstacle we cannot overcome
with the help of others.

Hypocrite

I want to expound on these definitions
so you know the difference.
Shall I commence with the evidence
about the pretense, intense,
overcome-tense --
there are three categories, so don't worry --
just pick and choose
what moves your groove.
I hope you take a little time
before this rhyme
blows your mind,
because I'm just tryin' to be kind
before you lose what little time
you have left,
so don't get mad, because I'm not sad.
Better grab that rag, wipe off your Bible,
because you need to hear about the Disciples;
they're not all the same,
and I'm trying to make it plain,
so dang, will you give me a chance
to talk about the romance of all three,
but we might not all agree,
that's okay, have it your way,
everybody has a different perception
about the resurrection.
My mama used to say "Rise and shine,"

and we would rise,
but there wasn't always a shine,
if you don't mind me saying.
I'm just trying to do a little persuasion,
and I hope this isn't a conflict of interest --
oh, did I already mention this?
Maybe I left out a little something,
but there's no need to rumble,
because all you have to do is become humble
before you crumble
under the pressure.
Have you ever done time in jail,
because a place of isolation
is not a good vacation,
or if that's not your situation,
then with your permission,
I'd like to add a new addition,
not aggression,
nor the new fashion,
but can you imagine having a passion
of things to come,
so you won't have to run, dummy,
because you're going to look like a mummy.
You're just a couple inches from the trenches,
so I'll catch you on the rebound,
how does that sound
for now?

Sinocrite

A sinocrite is a pretender,
so you'd better remember
to be careful
before you get your hand caught in that blender.
I hope you start praying
instead of saying
something you don't mean.

All you had to do was make it plain,
straightforward.
Don't try to fake me
or shake me loose,
like a blind goose going out to roost,
I just gave you a boost.

You've got to rise early
if you want to pull the wool
over my eyes,
so if I don't respond,
don't think that I'm dead
or metamorphosed,
because I will rise
to the occasion
with much revelation,
and all you will feel is the sensation.

Discernment is the key
to that remedy,
so go ahead
and keep it all movin' on
to a brand-new song.

Saintocrite

The intender possesses a little more wit --
he Ain't that quick,
but he thinks he's pretty slick.
He will confess, or even attest
to being the best,
because everything he does is with intent.

He's gonna lie, because he's got nothing
to lose.
His three-second fuse
is always giving everybody the blues —
this joker thinks he's got a four-leaf clover.

He needs a whole bunch of construction
from the inside out,
but even if there is a revolutionary change,
he'll keep playing the same old
game,
trying to stake his claim.

Saintocrite the overcomer
sounds like a real good fit,
because he Ain't about to trip,
it's all good, like it should,
healing for the soul, gold
for the mind,
all good things happen in time.

There are no shackles on the feet,
no cuffs on the hands,
that's what I recommend.
Can I have a hand, because that's fat, doc,
because his house is built on a foundation
that's solid as a rock

What I like about the Saintocrite
is that no matter how many times he falls,
grace will pick him up
and wash him off
as if he never failed.

Well, grace abounds
all over town, because his accusers accuse,
but he will be justified when Christ appears.
Oh my dear, the glorious fear
of the Lord
shall be his reward,
so these are the definitions of this condition,
and now that you know,
surely, you can go with the flow.

Lower Than Low

Some say you can only go so low,
and until you've been lower
than low,
there's nowhere else to go,
and you're at a dead end,
so don't forget about me,
because you see, I've been places
where there are no traces
of hope.

You always ask yourself "How did I get here?
How could this have happened?"
There are so many questions,
and so few answers.
The days are long,
as if you entered into eternity
with a death sentence,

and can I mention all the voices
that bring condemnation?
Delusions lead you to a place
where dishonor rules supremely,
and the only thing that stands out
are the mistakes
shaken by the wakening of trouble.

Lower than low
means you have no kind of flow,
and you feel like you could die,
but your cry
isn't heard by those closest to you,
but by Him who holds your destiny.

Sometimes the emotions
make you want to hide.
I've been shocked to the core,
wondering when the daylight will reappear —

lower than low is a place
where it's so dark, you wonder
if God Himself can see through
the thick layers of confusion.

If there's a lower than low, you think,
there has to be a higher than high,
where you can once again see the blue sky,
a new horizon
where the sun shines, and joy returns home;
where integrity rises to the occasion
and you are protected
by an unseen friend,
whose name is Jehovah-Nissi the God,
who goes before you in battle,
the God who looks ahead and provides,
because He knows
when His prizes should be encouraged.

He said He would never leave,
nor forsake you.
He will stay with you 'til the end,
when everything in your world has gone haywire,

so you should know
that He's always in control.
Let that be your hope for tomorrow,
because your sorrows
might endure for a night,
but joy will appear in the morning —
you've only just begun your journey,
so hold on, because the Master
will fulfill all your hopes and dreams.
I ask you to forgive me
for coming up short as a father.
I feel that I've failed, miserably,
and if I could turn back the hands of time,
I would ask God to grant me
one wish,
which would be to become the best father
in the world,
and my honest prayers are with you,
so we will weather life's storms together.
Hold on, stay strong,
and when we fall, we can always return
and rejoice
in the glory of the Father.

Oppressor Oppressed

The oppressor is the one
who forces others to do his bidding,
without concern for the welfare
of the individual.
No feels of remorse are required,
when it comes to the way others believe,
because trust is not needed
when you treat others like property.

The oppressor chooses to oppress,
because he feels he has the right to do
whatever he pleases.
He believes God granted him
special privileges,
free reign to do whatever.

The oppressed finds himself in a compromising position
where must choose to resists,
or submit to the harsh reality
that his life is going to be hell.
Resistance increases the chances of abuse,
both physically and verbally,
without any regard for individual rights.

The oppressor knows no boundaries
when it comes to dominating others,
just to gain free labor —

the difference between
the oppressor and the oppressed
is that only one of them
has the ability
to inflict harm
upon the other.

In Time

In time, all things will come to a pause,
and truth shall reveal itself
and bear the purpose
for which it exists.

Time is the revealer of all mysteries,
be it hidden or transparent.
Time has an expiration date
that always ends on time —
it moves at a pace
dictated by its own makeup,
it goes, moves, and flows,
and nobody really knows
the truth.

Time consists of seconds, minutes,
hours, days, months, years,
decades, centuries, and millenia,
and in time, all things unfold
into the greater scheme of things.

Time is a puzzle,
and as we put the pieces together,
we shall see the creative forces
painting a picture
no one has ever seen
or dreamt of before.

On the Verge Of

They're on the verge of fighting
over what seems to be a light situation,
but to them, it's a matter of survival.
Caught in the cycle of poverty
where there's no relief,
nothing to stop the oppression
or self-affliction.

The people struggle with the idea
that there are many doors of opportunity
that present themselves to everyone,
but in reality, those doors only open
for those who qualify for the prize
of ascending to prosperity.

Many are on the verge of
losing what little they have.
To be on the verge
it to be in a place people hate,
yet they tolerate the situation,
because they have families depending on them.
It is a place where pride is broken,
faith is shattered, dreams fade,
love becomes lust,
craving something that's unreal.

Being "on the verge of" means
a counterfeit is better than nothing.
Being "on the verge of" is a place
where violence lurks behind the door,
waiting for an opportunity
to be opened at the right time.
To be "on the verge of"
is to be in a place where anything can happen;
it is an uncertain area
for those unprepared to go to war.

Crisis

In a state of uncertainty
with no place to go,
no way to explain the emergency
taking place.
I'm seeking solutions,
all of which end in illusion,
leaving my mind riddled with confusion
with no conclusion.

While I muse
about answers beyond my reach,
I strive to stabilize
my vulnerable emotions.
I'm in a place
where I feel I've lost all human connection,
unable to adjust to a place
that feels safe.

Crisis brings a wave of adversities
which seem to be trials, tests
I'm unequipped to face.
It appears I don't have as much control
as I thought,
trying to buy myself more time
while trying to figure out my next move.

I slipped off the cliff of confusion,
not knowing which way to go,
so I just flowed down the stream of turmoil,
sinking deeper and deeper
into despair,
wondering if anyone cared.

A crisis is a situation
that pops up in your life
uninvited.

Sometimes we learn how to process
stressful situations,
and sometimes we don't —
unexpected trouble can be a blessing
in disguise, or a curse
unmasking its true colors.

Crises come and go,
and we must learn to access
the appropriate support groups
and the proper resources
if and when we fall prey
to life's unpredictable behaviors.

I Will Face

I will face every difficulty
with God by my side —
He walks with me through every battle.
He's the God who already looked ahead
and provided me
with everything I need to win.
No one can match His infinite power;
everyone and everything
must obey His every command.

I will face everything,
all the while trusting in His every Word.
It is through faith that I believe in Him,
and "he who cometh to God
must believe that He is a rewarder
to those who diligently seek Him."

When I face trials and temptations,
I will call upon Him,
morning, noon, and night,
for He will never sleep in my hour of need.
Everything shall come to pass
when I begin to pray,
because He will listen, and answer.

He is the source of my strength,
the love of my life,
the keeper of my soul
and protector of my destiny.
He loves me in spite of everything I am not,
and His love reaches beyond
my meager abilities,
so, perhaps you see why
I can face any adversity
with Him by my side,
for He has promised never to leave
or forsake me —
rather, He will be with me
until the very end.
He will never fail me.

He will help me triumph
in everything
I do.

My Heart

My heart is drawn to things
and people
that capture the inner yearning
of my ambition.

My humanity seeks knowledge;
it seeks to understand mysteries
that run contrary to the pain,
but I've learned that my heart
can be persuaded to take a detour
at the right bait.

I have a propensity
to always chase the unknown,
the forbidden fruit of dark truth.
The light in my heart
holds me in a place of purity
to avoid incarceration
in a prison of greed and cruelty.

I thirst for knowledge
that has the potential
to either elevate my spirit
to the highest plain of spirituality,
send my consciousness
into the abyss of complete darkness.

My mind is constantly challenged
by right and wrong choices,
good and evil.

There is a war
for the power of my heart
raging.

Hell

Hell is a lonely place —
there's no one to talk to,
no company,
only darkness.

They say misery loves company,
and at times, when life seems like hell,
everything that can go wrong
will go wrong.
Everything you don't want to happen
will happen,
and even if you try to avoid trouble,
trouble will follow you everywhere,
as if you wore a sign on your back
saying, "My name is trouble."

In hell, it seems as if every negative force
in the universe
gravitates towards you,
and though there may be
dark times ahead,
just know that if there is a hell,
then there must also be a Heaven.

Better or Bitter?

That is the choice on must make
when deciding how to respond
to life's many adversities.
In life, there will always be challenges, hardships,
differences of opinion,
and sometimes much tension,
but in order to retain your integrity,
you must continue to strive for excellence
in the midst of mistaken identity.

To label a person for his or her mistakes
is to judge
without knowing the whole story,
but then again, isn't that the norm
for society to strike before the fight?
If you defend your beliefs,
even if others don't agree,
then who shall have the last word?
You? God? A friend? Or an enemy?

I truly don't know,
but I do know
that to be bitter
means you are giving in to your enemy's plan
to strip you of all hope.

Bitterness has filled graveyards prematurely
with many broken spirits
who wished for a second chance.

Your choices will lead you
down one road or another,
but before you start down your path,
you need to ask yourself:
do I want to be bitter
or better?

I've Been Through

I've been through recession, depression, and
other things you couldn't possibly
imagine.

I've walked through the valley
of the shadow of death;
I've been through rain, storms, snow,
sleet, so, do you still doubt me?

I've been through incarceration,
and I understand the process of emancipation,
freedom from the darkness that pursued me.

I recognize that I'm free,
because now I can truly see.
The light has come,
my mind is illuminated,
my ways consecrated
as I walk life's path.

The stain of glory
is my victorious story
about what I've been through,
how I've overcome,
and how deeply I know
how it feels to triumph
over the darkness.

Don't Hit My Mama!

Don't hit my mama, you bully! You know
you're too big to be punchin' her
with them big hands.
If you slap my mama one more time,
I'm gonna find somethin'
to hurt you with
like you hurt her.
I don't know why
a big, ugly man like you
would hit a woman — you're nothin'
but a coward,
because I don't see you beating a man like that.

If I was your size,
I'd beat you down to the ground
for what you've done.
I'm too little to fight back; all I can do
is scream and holler,
hoping you'll honor my cries for mercy.

You're gonna kill my mama,
if you keep hittin' her like that.
Just wait until I'm all grown up;
I'll beat the hell out of you, I swear,
because I'll never forget the look of anguish
and helplessness
on my mama's face.

How could you hurt the person
who gave you a child?

I don't understand; do you want me to grow up
and become an abuser of women
or an advocate
for them?

In Prison

Sitting here in this prison,
I'm wondering how I ended up here,
and as I begin to reflect,
I remember warning signs
that I did not heed,
and I feel remorse
for my wild and reckless behaviors
that did nothing but hurt others.

Everyone I knew tried everything
humanly possible
to stop me from falling into the abyss
of incarceration,
and sitting here now,
I now see everything I could have done
differently,
but I was wild, moving towards my own demise,
and now all I can do is wonder
how the hell did I end up here?

I, and I alone, had the power
to make different choices along the way,
and now that I've crossed the line,
I wonder if it's too late
to change my ways.

Some lessons we only learn through suffering,
and now my options are few and far between —
I created a nightmare
that should have been a dream,
and now that I can reflect on my past
and look ahead into my own future,
I can, finally, make
an informed choice.

In There

In there waits a small boy
struggling along his journey to manhood,
only he can't seem to overcome
all the obstacles in his path.
I see cuts and bruises on his soul,
as if he's been traumatized
by a set of strange hands
that stole his ability to grow normally.

In there lies a man
who still looks like a little boy,
because he never matured; he is out of touch
with reality,
detached from human connection —
all he has ever known
is misery.

In there waits a man
who was born for greatness,
who has not yet come to realize
his own destiny,
but in time, he will rise to the occasion.

He will push beyond his fears.
He will dare his darkness
to hold him back.

He has tasted freedom,
and that freedom
has given him the strength
to dare to become whole
again.

Perpetrate

Perpetrate is just another concentrate
of ignorance,
put upon a generation of unsuspecting youth
who don't know what to do.
If they would listen,
they wouldn't regret the past so much,
and now they must pay their dues to society,
because Ain't nothin' for free.

Life was not meant to be hard,
but if you play the wrong cards,
it's going to be crazy,
so don't even think about being lazy —
if you had a job, you wouldn't have robbed
yourself of life, liberty,
and the pursuit of happiness,
and now you're feeling sad,
because you committed yourself
to a life of atrocity.

It's not because of your class
or social status,
and you'd better realize
that there is a grand prize
for those who show common sense
as they strive for excellence.

Don't get caught up in all the hype,
because pretty soon you'll be out of sight,
trying to fight
with a grain of sand,
you're still sinking, man,
so take my advice
and think twice
before you decide to roll those dice,
because you could lose everything,

so don't let perpetration
be your decimation,
but your consecration.

The Chameleon Syndrome

I became a chameleon
to survive the onslaught of those
who look upon me with jealousy, hatred,
and deceit,
because they can't compete
with their own insecurity.

They frown like the clown called "King,"
like some nightmarish dream,
which is just a scheme
as they work to find a way
to make me fall from greatness,

but they don't have the power,
so they put up this facade,
speaking lies, until their eyes
turn pitch-black
before they attack.

Sometimes we have to become someone else
to escape the clutches of bondage.
The chameleon syndrome is a survival tactic
to escape the insurmountable hatred
from others.

We learn how to deal with negative people;
we learn how to prevent their
detrimental behaviors
from decimating our lives
with their twisted
and poisoned philosophy.

The Fight

There's a fight for my will
raging inside,
and I feel the turmoil within my soul
seeking a place of peace;
I see humanity crying out to be free,
but I feel powerless
to bring change to a dying race.

I'm not sure how things will turn out,
but without a shadow of a doubt,
He is more than able
to help me succeed
in turning lives around for the greater good.

This fight is designed to bring me
to the next level; it builds character
and resiliency.

If I am going to overcome
insurmountable odds,
I must learn how to stand my ground
and move beyond mediocrity
into greatness.

I will not allow myself
to sit idly by
and do nothing.

I am determined
not to lose this fight,
but to win.

This Brown Skin

At times, this brown skin has been looked upon
with disdain.
I feel the pain through the words
and looks
of the others who try to fold me
into their little world of insignificance,
but there's no evidence
that I'm anything less than great.

This brown skin
is one-sixteenth of an inch thick,
painted with the essence of my existence,
because I matter.

Others have been battered
by negative vibes that breathe lies
with their fly-by-night misconceptions
but the Creator painted my silhouette
with a beautiful brown hue
without all the blues,

and I won't respond to them,
because I know my worth
is greater than the dirt
they spew from their tongue.
Not knowing their own self-worth,

they continue to hurt others,
their estranged brothers,

but I'm proud to be brown,
that's just how I get down,
by being myself
and holding my head up high.
I will always be looking to the sky,
because the sky's the limit,

and therefore,
I will soar into the heavens
like an hawk —
this brown skin
is the only tool I have
to reveal the true me
as I walk around in complete
liberty.

Tranquility

I'm allowing my mind to take the time
to de-stress from this busy day
of dealing with humanity.
Tranquility allows the mind to reassess solutions
for conflict
and bring peace to troubling lives.

Tranquility is learning problem-solving techniques
meant to calm a mind
moving at the speed of life out of control,
taking a time-out
in order to move back into the balance,
an equilibrium
where life is on an even plane.

Tranquility means knowing
that you have the option
to take the higher road to liberation
without contemplation,
knowing that the confirmation
in your own heart
will guide you through life's stormy seas.

Tranquility means reducing strife,
and knowing
that everything
is going to be alright.

U Left Too Soon

Pops, you know I love you, man,
and I know life had a plan,
but you left too soon; we never got to talk
like a father and son should have.
We never played sports
like a man raising a son should have,
and now I'm all alone
with no one to share my problems with.
I'm drowning in my tears; my heart is filled with fear.
all because you left a little too soon.
A little too soon, a little too soon,
a little too soon, a little too soon,
a little too soon, a little too soon.
You left a little too soon,
before I became a man.
You waited a little too late to say *I love you*.
Pops, I know you loved me —
you showed me,
and I truly believe you were the greatest dad
on Earth.
You were my superstar,
and by far, I wanted to be just like you when I grew up,
but now my heart is filled sorrow,
and you know tomorrow is my birthday.
I will have to celebrate without you,
but it won't be the same,

now that you're gone.
You waited just a little too late
to leave this place without saying goodbye.
My eyes are filled with tears, my heart still prays
that you will one day come back.
Pops, I will always love you,
and now there's no trace of your smile
whenever I need your grace to help me through another day.
Pops, you left a little too soon,
a little too soon,
a little too soon,
a little too soon.

Wanted

She wanted to be free, yet she didn't possess
the rights of freedom.

Incapacitated by the dastardly deeds
of the master, his only desire
was to force his darkest folly upon on her,
but even that could not kill her will
to be free.
She saw that her body
was nothing more than a toy
to him,
and every day, he spoke to her
with words of hate,
yet she dreamed of being loved,
of not being used and abused.

She was born into a world where she was purchased
for just a few dollars
to the highest bidder at an auction,
all her goods on public display
so that others could look upon their investment.

It seemed as life
wasn't stacked in her favor,
but she dreamed of finding a savior
who would set her free
from the men who killed her dream.

All she had to keep her hope alive
was the dream
that one day she would be released from bondage
and live free,
just like all the others.

Hypocrisy

Hypocrisy
is when words are spoken in ignorance
due to one's own bias.

People pretend to be human,
when in reality,
they possess the heart of a beast.
Their animalistic nature
causes them to act as if
they don't know any better,
but truth be told,
death is staring them right in the face.

People act like God has chosen them
over all others,
and like actors, they put on a good show
before men,
but their words are poisonous.
They smile, but that is a cover-up
to hide the intentions
of their dark hearts.

They are nothing but two-faced personalities,
mixing truth and lies together,
and the listener should beware

of the hypocrisy
these people speak,
because it is never, ever
the truth.

After the Dance

After 28 years of marriage,
she decided to let it go completely.
She dreamt of being loved
unconditionally.

Her life had taken a few twists
and turns,
leaving behind broken hearts
and delayed dreams.
After years of unseen love, she feels a longing
for the promise
made at the beginning of courtship
that was never kept.

Love should know no boundaries,
but this time, it did,
and now that she music has stopped,
she must begin to rebuild
this broken bridge.

After so many painful years, she is stronger
than she could have ever imagined.
Now it's time for her to transition
to a strange, yet familiar place
where promises are kept.

Her life is far from over; her desires
still burn within her heart,
and she is beginning a new journey,
released from incarceration,
and, set free, she will gravitate
towards someone
who loves her
unconditionally.

Brother Down

You can't hold a good brother down —
he's been around too long,
he's seen all the games you play.
He'll catch you comin' through the back door,
he's hip to your tricks.
Don't underestimate him,
because Ain't nothing for free,
so you've gotta get real,
because he's worked too hard to get scammed.

You can't keep a good brother down,
but you can take his job; you can
repossess his car,
steal his house,
but he'll rise again, because his eyes
are on the prize,
and he believes in his dreams.
His inner power sustained him
through his darkest hours,
so don't be sour
if you can't bring a good man down.

A good brother walks with the Savior,
and even if he's found guilty
of any crime,
he will be exonerated over time,
because he is destined to become great,
so stay out of his way -- nothing
will keep him away from his dreams.

I can't say enough about the good brother,
except to tell him to keep pushing on
until another brother needs
a wise and strong helping hand.

Combat Ready

It's been said that if you stay ready,
you never have to *get* ready,
because we live in a world
that is always on Defcon 1.
We have become nations of warmongers,
looking for the slightest opportunity
to inflict destruction
upon our brothers
without regret.

If there are no voices of reason,
we will soon become
extinct,
yet we are indifferent,
and at times, we can't even find a middle ground
to agree upon.

We retreat to safe places
and withdraw our weapons
to try and prove that we're right
and the other person is wrong,
but nothing real is accomplished,
so we keep our defenses up
on high alert.

When will we learn from our past mistakes?
History repeats itself
when the lessons of life and love
are ignored by power-hungry men.
Instead of combat ready, I wish us to become
"love ready,"
so that we may put down our arms
and live in peace.

Fashioned by the Hand of God

They were fashioned by the Hand of God,
and they bear the mark of their Savior
upon their spirits,
a notice to all that they have been given
Royal approval.

The cross permits them to move
through other realms,
taking souls without a moment's notice.
They, too, were once broken by this life,
until the Master healed them
and removed the darkness from their lives.

They possess the authority of the Spirit of God,
and they fight day and night.
When they pray, the Host of Heaven
stands, ready to do battle
with the spoken Word of God
as a shield.

They are fierce in prayer,
and all they have to do is say, "Jesus,"
and all the weaker powers cower in fear.

They are the warriors of God,
chosen to do battle on the field
where men were made from clay.

They were washed in the Blood of Christ,
and now they are strong enough
to pull lost souls back
into the marvelous light of God.

In the end, they will always win
because Jesus is their eternal friend.

I Refuse!

I refuse to live
as if there were no hope, happiness,
peace, or joy.
I refuse to live as if I were broke,
busted, and unable to be trusted
by those who consider me a threat.
I refuse to not to enjoy the fruits
of my independence.
I refuse to say "Yes, sir,"
unless I have the freedom to say "No."
I refuse to believe anything is impossible.
I refuse to believe that I am destined to fail.
I refuse to lie down and surrender,
because I've been knocked down
hundreds of times,
and each time I'd stood back up.

Victory is achieved
by refusing to give up,
by keeping hope alive,
and by continuing to trust
in what I know to be real.

Every obstacle is here
for a brief moment of time,
and I refuse
to let any obstacle
beat me.

Nothing to Fear

You have nothing to fear.
Having fear
means believing that there is a possibility
that you will be hurt
by the one you love.
Fear only arises when distrust
rears its ugly head
and tries to intimidate the one
who holds the key to God's true nature.

We only fear
because we've been taught,
through negative experiences
that leave us uncertain, constantly wondering
whether the next recipient of our love
is for real.

We must learn to discern,
learn how to work through difficult situations
that seem to emulate previous relationships.

Love is designed to endure
the most painful, heart-wrenching events
in a person's life,
and no matter how long it takes,
love will always rise
like a blazing sun
to heal all our disappointments.

There's No

There's no partiality with God,
although it often seems as if
He doesn't hear my screams
or pay attention to my dreams,
but life is not fair, and I'm quite aware
of that, but the fact remains
that I struggle to stay sane,
and at times, I want to blame someone else
for my pain.

I've often asked, "Why is there so much suffering
in my life?"
As I continue to pray, I'm seeking truth
that seems to be hiding from me.
I'm trying to understand
the true master plan,
but time and time again, I come up empty.

Deep down in my heart,
I know that He is merciful
and just, but I must trust
that He will never leave me
nor forsake me,
that He will stay with me
until the very end, and though sometimes His love is silent,

I have dreams of being made whole,
and I know everything will be alright,
because in God, there is no partiality;
there is only redemption.

The Lies of Men

History declares that men
who thirst for power
will eliminate everything and everyone
in their way
on the road to domination —
I have seen the complete annihilation
of races, cultures, and indigenous peoples
for the purpose of
selfish and destructive plans.

These men have become codependent,
living off the unsubstantiated statements
they continue to spew
over television, radio, and social media,
spitting sensationalist lies
in order to convince the audience
that these crimes against humanity
are justified.

They say they have sworn on oath
to serve the people,
but their forked tongues
speak no truth,
and instead, spread propaganda,

but one day, these corrupt men
will be put on trial,
and truth will win in the end.

In the land of men,
and under the holiest of judgments,
these liars will swear
to tell the truth, the whole truth,
and nothing but the truth,
so help them God.

Judas Heart

Like Judas, he pretended to be a friend,
while all along, hatching an evil plan.
He talked right, he acted right
around others,
until he met the ones who were
hateful brothers.

Hell hath no treachery
like a man wanting his way,
and little does he know
that the seeds he sows
will not only affect him,
but those he claims to love most.

The consequences of having a hardened heart
is that you lose all common sense,
which only leads to emptiness.

Judas treachery will lead him down a path
of no return,
and the deal to betray someone
is written in blood,
and a Judas heart will betray you
for money, fame, or power,
only to find out, once it's too late,
that he's selling his soul to the Devil himself.

The heart of Judas will consume
anyone who is greedy,
because greed knows no boundaries.
The root of all evil is not money,
but the worship of money,
and Judas' love for money was far greater
than his desire for friendship.

I can't imagine being betrayed by the one
who professed to be my friend,
only to make a deal with my enemies
behind my back,

but an opportunist will always take advantage
of any situation.

A Judas heart always believes
that it is innocent,
free and clear
of the innocent blood on their hands,

but blood can never be wiped clean
completely,
because it always leaves
a stain.

The Power of Consent

Jesus said, "No man may take my life freely,
I lay it down,"
and the crowd was surprised,
thinking they'd have to take the King of Kings
by force,
but it would be His ultimate choice
to willingly die for sinners like us.

On his walk to the cross, He laid
a plan in motion,
a plan that would destroy his enemies' game
to bring shame, and blame,
back on the liar's name.
He would take sin, transgression,
and inquiries,
and nail them to the wood,
crucifying it with blood
and quieting the voices of the accusers
who blamed the people before God.

It was His choice to go to that cross
and appease the Father.
Empowered by the Holy Ghost,
He would journey to the bowels of hell,
where he would preach

for three days and three nights,
proclaiming that He was the Christ,
and on the third day, He rose,
declaring, "I am alive,"

A Sense of Loss

A sense of loss — losing something that's so near
and dear to the heart,
leaving behind a trace of essence,
marking history as a person
who made an indelible mark
upon the lives of those who are intimately acquainted
with the personal touch
of being important.

A sense of loss — reflecting upon the good times,
remembering special moments
and pleasant times in order to hang on to hope.

A sense of loss — losing moments
of friendly gatherings,
only to appreciate them a little more
upon reflection,

A sense of loss
is more than just a notion.
Memories fade, they come and go,
but the seasons that have gone by
serve as sweet inspiration,
moments to be treasured

by all who know and care about
that particular individual,
giving way to freedom as we know it,
and now that sense of loss
becomes a sense of gain.

Left to Myself

If I was left to myself, my world
would spiral out of control,
coated by the taste of folly,
packed with unlimited freedom
to do as I pleased
without restrictions or limitations
imposed upon me.

If I was left to myself, *too much*
would never be enough.
Too little would a crime,
as my mind took its greedy time
to devour everything in sight.
My plight would be one
of endless indulgence,
and I would enjoy every moment
of my darkness.

If I was left to myself, everything
would be all about me,
and I would have no need
for assistance; I would be free
to take as I pleased,
and there would be no asking,

only taking, pillaging, stealing.
I would commit crimes all the time
without worrying about serving time,
because there is no one to arrest the criminal
when he is left to himself.

Alternate Reality

I'm living in a surrealistic reality,
trying to change my dimension,
wondering why I can't move beyond
this state of being,
feeling déjà vu over and over again.

It's almost as if I walked into
a parallel dimension
where my path has led me
into the negative side,
and while I'm struggling along my path,
I look to the other side
and watch my other self
going about his way
on the positive side.

I long to turn my nights
into days, my pain into joy,
despair into hope,
disappointments into expectation,
my brokenness into healing,
and yet I must continue to achieve
to pursue the indomitable dream
stirring within my heart.

I see two realities:
one chases me, and the other,
I chase.

Lonely Walk

I've been through some low spots
on this lonely road called life.
The search for happiness
has been an elusive dream
at times,
but I kind of understand that walking alone
means that I am in
a vulnerable state
where I'm defenseless
against the endless onslaughts of depression
trying to kill my joy.

Life is a packaged deal
that comes with a variety of tests,
trials, and uncertainties,
with no guarantee of a happy ending,
but still, I must fight
with all my might
to survive this lonely war
known only to humanity.

When Facing a Mountain

When you're facing a mountain,
you must hope that your mountain-mover
to lead you through, around,
and over the obstacles
standing in your way.

You must keep your eyes upon Him,
and although, at times,
it seems difficult to trust Him,
you must remember
that He has promised never to abandon
or forsake you.

Often, we wonder why
God leads us through certain hills and valleys
we are not familiar with —
it's frightening to be led down unknown trails.
During those moments
when you feel most vulnerable,
you must walk closer to God,
and even though you cannot see
past the mountain,
you must trust that He
is in full control over your destiny.

We might not always know why
the Father does what He does,
but we must believe
that He will never give us more hardship
than we can bear.

When facing a mountain,
look to the Father, and He will show you
how to climb it.

God wishes to share His strength
with you,
and we must whole-heartedly believe
in the things we cannot see,
for God rewards
those who seek Him.

When facing your next mountain,
call the Father's name,
and he will answer.

No Other Recourse

I have no other recourse, but to stand
against all who oppose me.

I have been forced into a corner
with no choice but to move forward
towards my ultimate objective.

I've been taught the art of war,
I've learned how to overcome
the many obstacles and challenges
threatening my survival,
and I must stay strong
and fight against the insurmountable pressures
trying to defeat me.

I must unleash my weapon
of mass success
and use tactical strategies
to neutralize each and every enemy
challenging my right to rule victorious
over my own life.

I must obliterate every negative thought
that opposes me.
I must win the war for myself.

In the Depths

In the depths of my pain,
there seems to be no relief
in sight.

My soul voices the need for
deliverance,
and I wonder how I can possibly
escape from this imprisonment
and move forward,

away from a place
that is trying to kill my belief
there is a utopia
somewhere out there,
a place where there is no doubt,
no reservation, no fear, pain,
or darkness.

My only hope
is that I will survive the pain,
so that I can be of service
to others who feel lost, hopeless,
and trapped in the depths
of their own pain.

Recidivism

I feel recidivated, incarcerated in my mind,
can't find the time to escape
to another place where freedom reigns.

I often dream
of living in a state of mind
where I am not bound
to my self-destructive behaviors,
and I can't figure out
how to correct my path.

I gamble with the idea
that if I take some chances
and move beyond my fears,
there may be a paradise
waiting just for me,
once I learn how to alter my mindset
and begin taking bold steps
forward.

It was the unknown I feared most,
and if I want to achieve my dreams,
I must contend
with my own lack of understanding.

Souls Passing Over

I heard the cries of souls passing over
to the other side.
Some of them cried, asked why they had to die,
while others just smiled and didn't ask anything.
The souls passing over gained some knowledge
while living in our material world,
but would that knowledge be enough
to secure them a home in the heavens?
The greatest of all fears
is the fear of the unknown,
and as I lie in bed, trying to sleep,
I hear their voices,
wondering where their soul's destination
will be.
I know they were only seeking hope
for a better life;
I can feel their joy, and their pain,
and like a bird ascending,
they are rising into the sky,
but those who wasted precious time
and trusted in lies descended,
as if the weight of the world
rested upon their shoulders —
they fled from the light.
There's something about the light
that doesn't run from darkness.

Darkness is always consumed
by the light,
and we are created with knowledge
that can either bless or curse us.
In this short life, we can choose to build
or dismantle, to give or take, love or hate,
but the choice is ours,
and when it comes our time to pass,
what will we say
in those moments
as we slide into eternity?

Triggers

Triggers are simply reminders
of something that happened in the past
that brought much pain
and disgrace,
and you must face your situation
in the wake of some potential shame.

Now you resent what happened,
but your enemies who wronged you
don't care about the consequences
of their actions upon you.

In their minds,
they are filled with rage,
and they believe you deserved punishment.
Like caged animals,
they only want to cause bloodshed.
It's callous, cold-hearted,
but it's the only way they can function,
and they will fight to the better end
to defend their beliefs,
and they will not be appeased
until your voice is silenced forever.

They want to be free of the memory
of you,

because all they remember is you
were a fool tryin' to be cool
but ended up dead,
because you forgot to pray to the God of Heaven
before you made a stupid mistake,
and now it's too late
to turn back the hands of time
and change your mind —
what happened has now been written in stone:

Here lies a man
who took the wrong road
and ended up in the dead lane.

It doesn't take much to trigger someone; just remind them
of a perceived injustice,
and they will be quick to cast judgment,
without ever giving a second thought
to what their lives could be,
until they are free from the one who caused them
so much misery.